My Two Feet on the Ground

By Leanne Costello

A fun, rhyming book for children
on positivity and mindfulness

Balboa Press books may be ordered through booksellers or by contacting:

Balboa Press
A Division of Hay House
1663 Liberty Drive
Bloomington, IN 47403
www.balboapress.com.au
AU TFN: 1 800 844 925 (Toll Free inside Australia)
AU Local: 0283 107 086 (+61 2 8310 7086 from outside Australia)

Illustrations by Leanne Costello

ISBN: 978-1-5043-2156-3 (sc)
ISBN: 978-1-5043-2157-0 (e)

Print information available on the last page.

Balboa Press rev. date: 02/24/2023

My Two Feet on the Ground

For Mum and Dad

First day at school, I am new
And everyone around,
Is looking at me, but that's okay
My feet are on the ground.

I feel my back, straight and tall
I see it in my mind.
We're all children in a classroom
And we're all one of a kind.

Lunch time bell, sit in the sun
Making friends takes time.
My face is warm, my tummy's full
And soon it will be home-time.

Welco

If I feel lost and all alone, I take a look around –
I am here,
I am safe
With my two feet on the ground.

I had a little fight today,
It made me very sad.
I think that I have hurt their feelings
And I wish I never had.

How can I move on from this?
I don't know where to start.
Next time I'll think, before I act
And say sorry from my heart.

Walking under frosty skies
For fun and exercise,
Breathing cold air in and hot steam out
Just like a kettle spout!

We're home again with nice hot drinks
My cheeks are red and rosy.
The dog's asleep on my two feet,
Feeling warm and cosy.

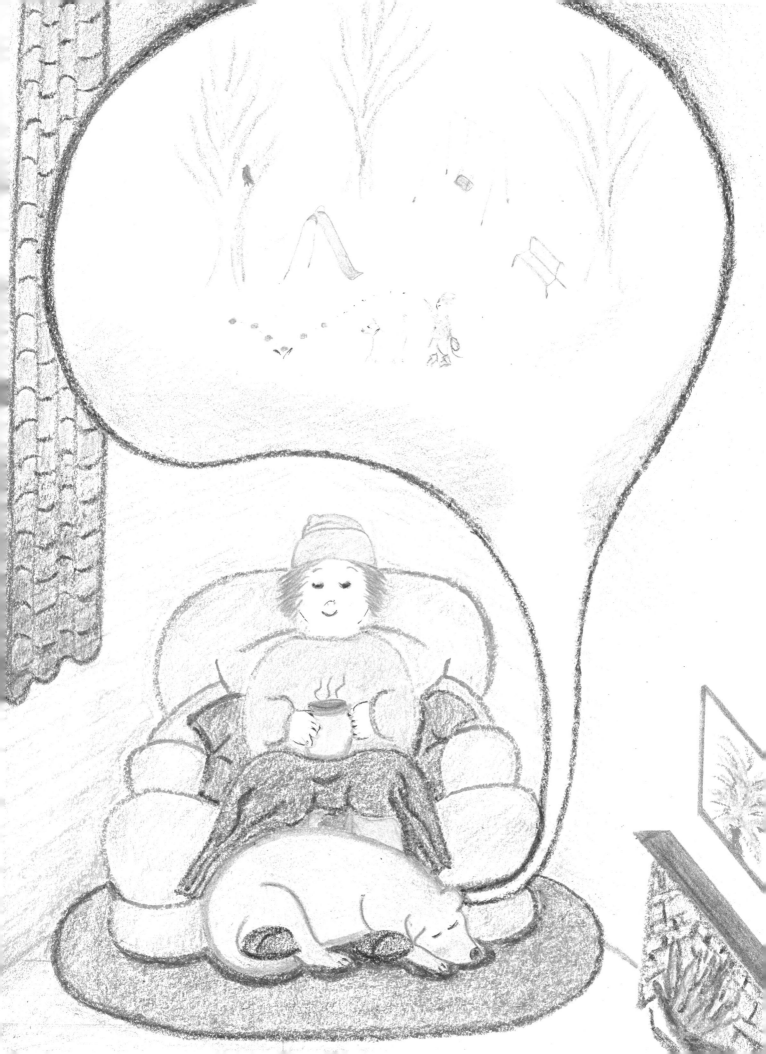

I feel sick and can't eat breakfast,
So no school for me today.
But with some rest and medicine
I'll soon be on my way.

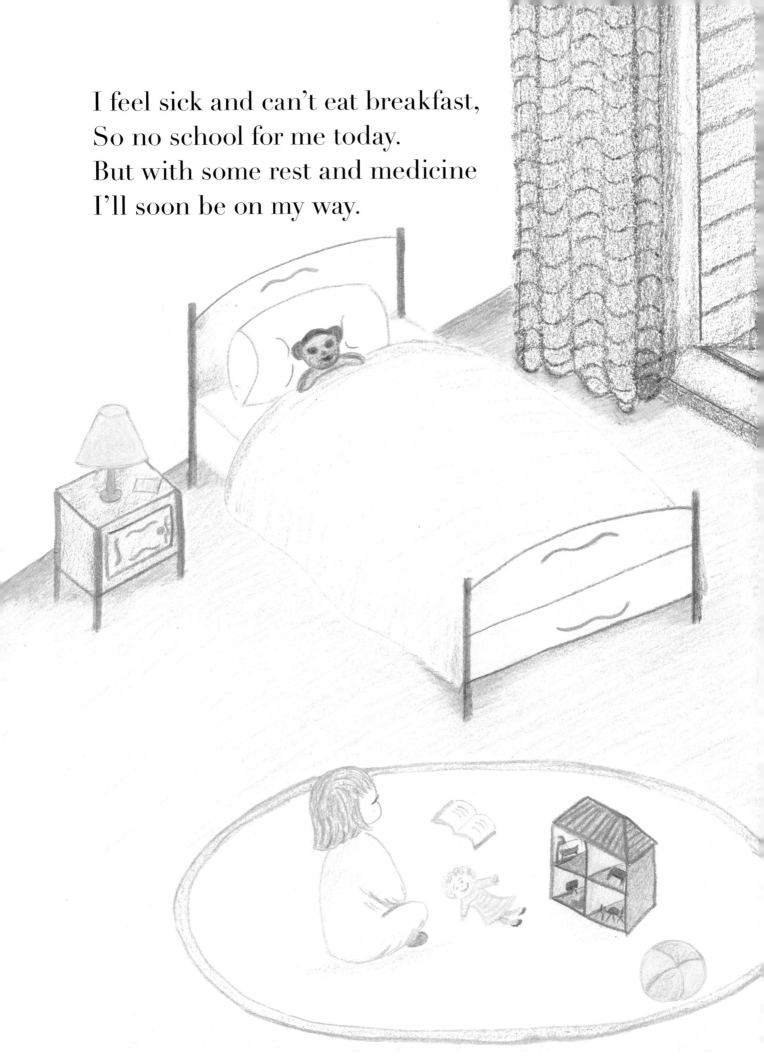

The falling rain sounds like music
While I'm playing with my toys.
It is simple things, which often bring
Comfort, fun and joy.

I sometimes turn the TV off
To hear the peace and quiet.
Five minutes rest is all it takes,
I recommend you try it!

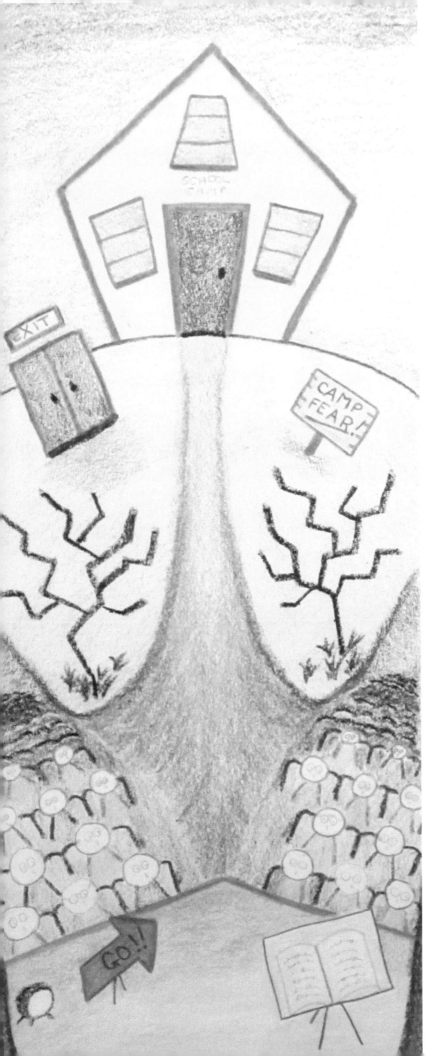

My first school camp
and I'm not sure
I really want to go.
The teachers will look
after me
And I'll be fine, I know.

It's like before my big
school concert,
When I am full of doubt.
I'll be myself and think
good thoughts,
Because it will all work out.

An exciting bus trip to our camp,
There's nature all around.
Then down the steps –
One, two, jump!
My feet land on the ground.

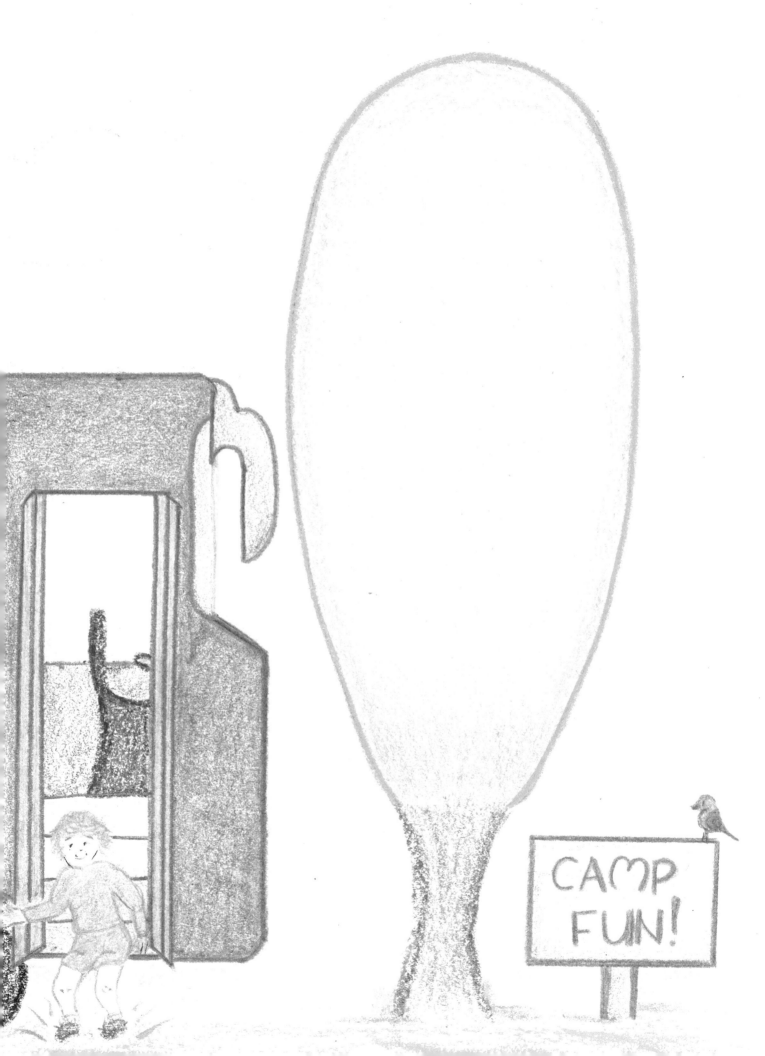

Rocks and pebbles, shrubs and trees,
There is not a sound –
Until I crunch the twigs and leaves
With my two feet on the ground!

Home again with big warm hugs,
Also from my sister.
I tell her about the fun on camp
And even that I missed her.

Now at a birthday party with kids I haven't met before.
I smile and think,
We're all unique
And feel my feet upon the floor.

Happy faces, games to play
And right before our eyes,
There's yummy cakes and mini pies!
It's fun to socialise.

There's a big school test, I studied well
But I have butterflies.
With self-belief I'll do my best
And grow up to be wise.

I'm just a kid, but I can see
Some things are worth achieving,
Like happiness,
Being your best
And never stop believing!

It's school sports day and it's okay,
To not always be the best.
You cannot win in everything,
But you can still be the fairest.

We all possess our special gifts,
They are inside to be found.
So follow your own special path,
With your two feet on the ground.

School holidays for me and you
Playing computer games.
The sun is out,
It seems a shame,
There must be something else to do.

Riding my bike is what I like –
I am adventure bound!
Pick up the pace,
Wind in my face,
My pedals spinning 'round!

Time for fun, we're at the beach,
The waves are pounding down
And the sand is cool and soothing
To my two feet on the ground.

It's shopping day, put our seatbelts on
Then all drive into town.
The sun shines on the asphalt carpark.
Hot feet on the ground!

The moon is up, I say goodnight
And climb underneath the doona.
I cannot sleep,
So I count sheep
And fall asleep much sooner!

Sometimes you can feel far away,
Floating like a star.
Just close your eyes and look inside
To see where and who you are.

What did I do today?

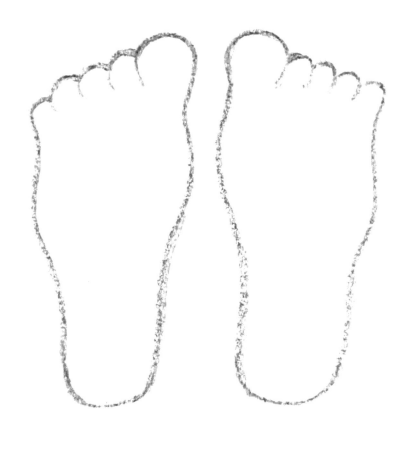

_____ _____ _____

_____ _____ _____

_____ _____ _____

_____ _____ _____

_____ _____ _____

.

Printed in the United States
by Baker & Taylor Publisher Services